CHAPTER ONE

Sex for Beginners

Simple ways to get it on AKA have a hump
AKA hide the salami AKA bump and grind.

1   Slip and Slide

2 Humpty Dumpty

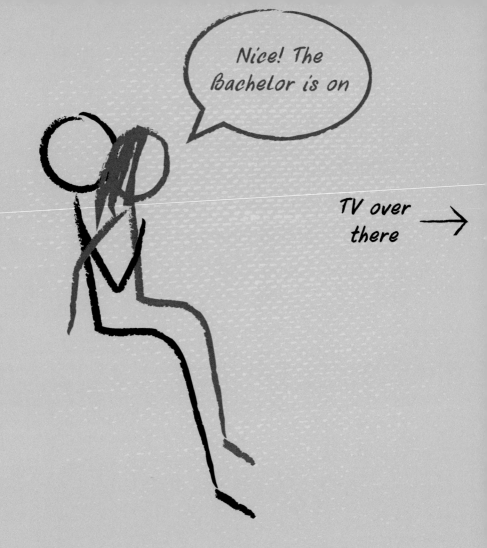

3 **If it Fits, I Sits**

4 Just the Dip

Easier if you're a
Russian ballerina →

5 **A Leg Up**

6 The Inspector Gadget

7   **Knocking on the Back Door**

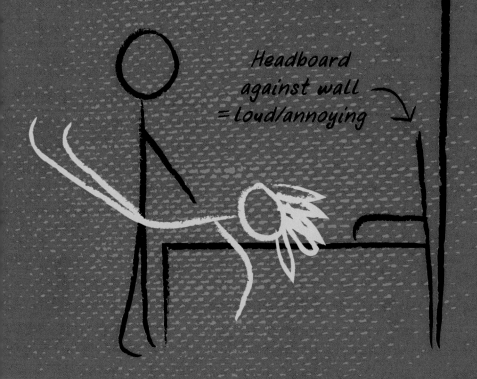

8 Bad Neighbors

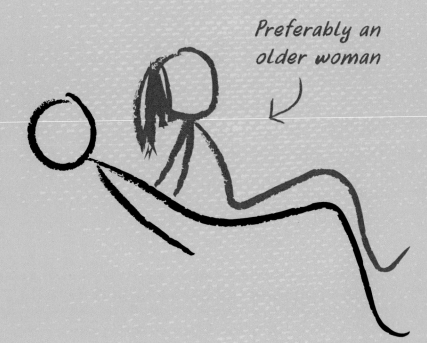

Preferably an older woman

COUGAR SIGHTED

9 | **Stacy's Mom**

Break down that wall! Like the Berlin wall except way less serious

10   **The Boner-Wall**

11 **The Wishboner**

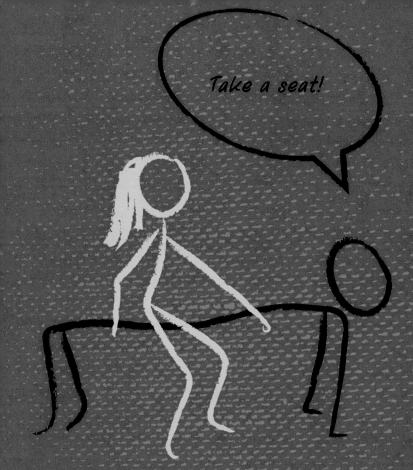

12 **The Park Bench**

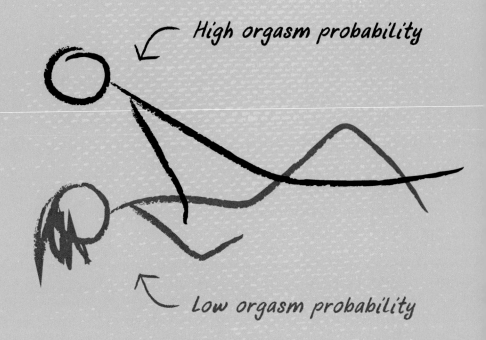

High orgasm probability

Low orgasm probability

13 **Boring But Effective**

GREATEST BONER EVERRRRRRRRR

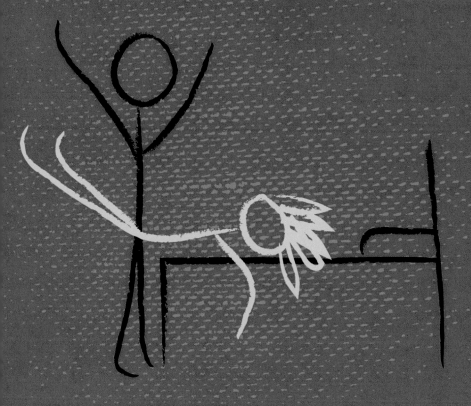

14 Erectile Disfunction Medication #1

Sad face

Worst boner ever

15 **Erectile Disfunction Medication #2**

Vibrator
named
Stefano

Probability of orgasm: 99%

16 **Girl's Best Friend**

Expert Tip: Use the left hand and it feels like you have a new girlfriend

17 Guy's Best Friend

Must have no fear, get right in there

18   **The Brown Noser**

CHAPTER TWO

Sex for The More Advanced

Slightly more challenging ways to stuff the turkey AKA know someone Biblically AKA do the disappearing cane trick AKA feed the kitty.

19 The Peacock

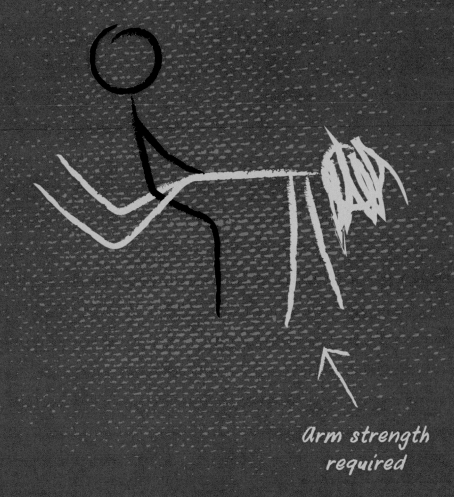

Arm strength required

20 Wheelbarrow Race

The stronger the pole the better

↑

Enough friction to
start an orgasm fire

21 **Pitching a Tent**

Requires serious boner strength

22 Look Ma, No Hands!

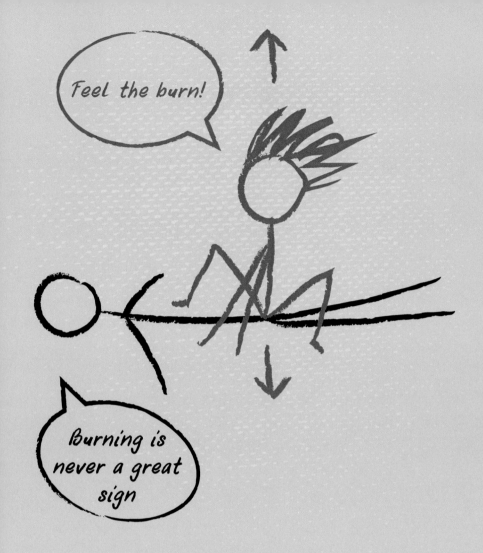

23   **The Thigh Master**

Not really sure how this works...

24 X's and Big O's

Great ab
workout

25 | **Standing Warm Pretzel**

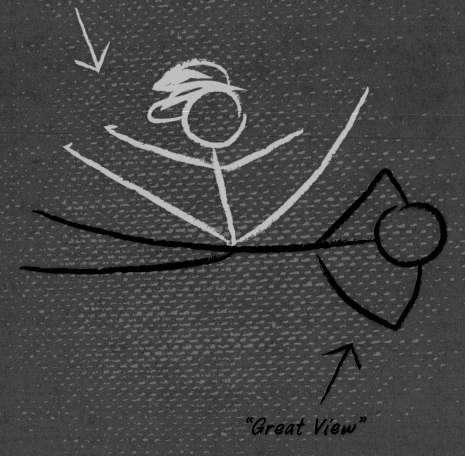

26 Banana Split

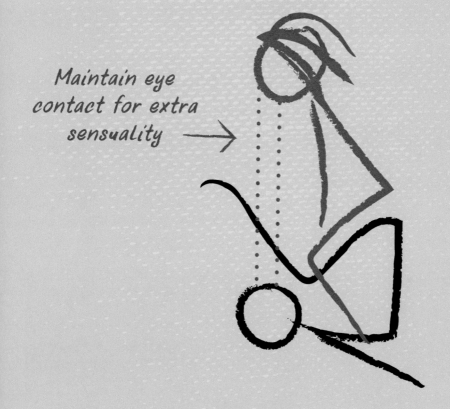

Maintain eye contact for extra sensuality →

27 Dick in a Box

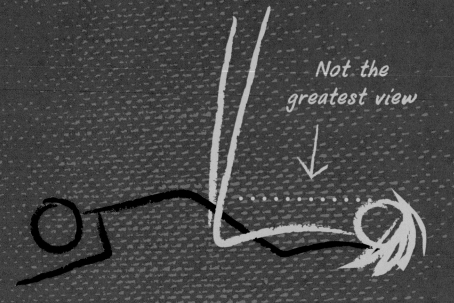

Not the greatest view

28 **Risky Business**

Flapping
recommended

29 | **I Believe I Can Fly**

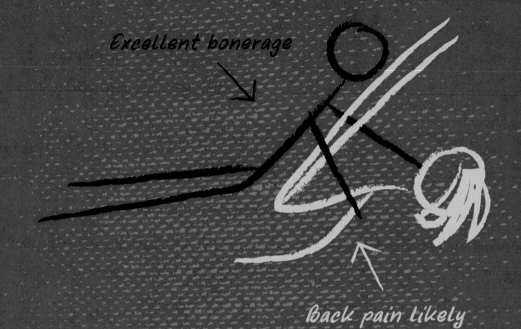

30   **The Deep End**

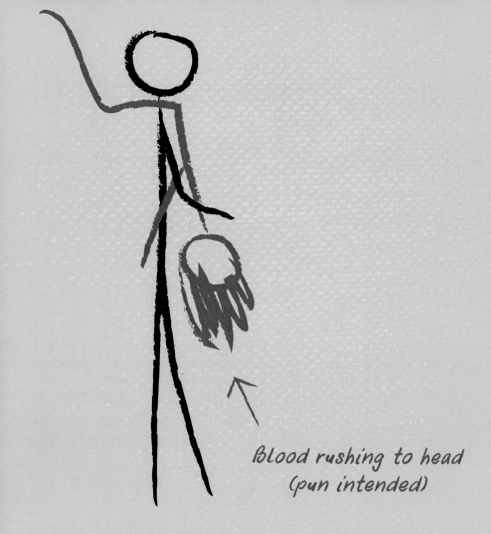

*Blood rushing to head
(pun intended)*

31 | **The Flying 69**

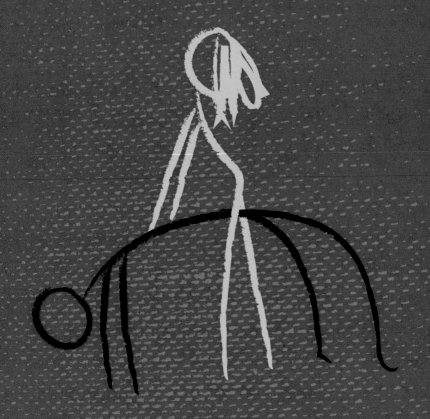

No chance this boner is falling down

32 London Bridge

CHAPTER THREE

For Sexperts

Complex ways to put a banana in the fruit salad AKA do the bedroom rodeo AKA launch the meat missile AKA do the midnight jockey ride AKA open the gates of Mordor AKA take the bald-headed gnome for a stroll in the misty forest.

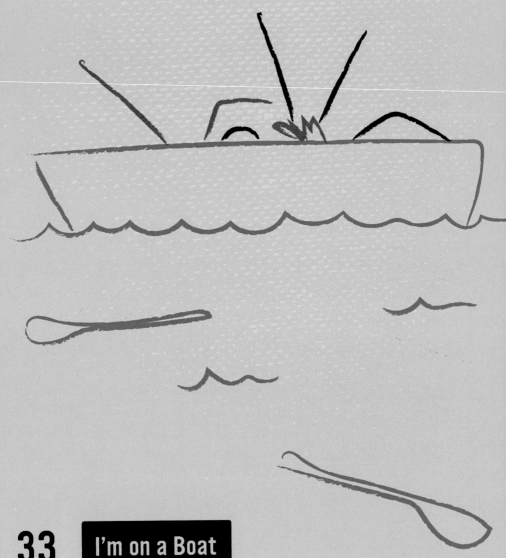

33 | I'm on a Boat

risk of rugburn

Monsters don't go bump in the night, these guys do

34 The Stairmaster

Anytime is a good time for this position

35 Sex O'Clock

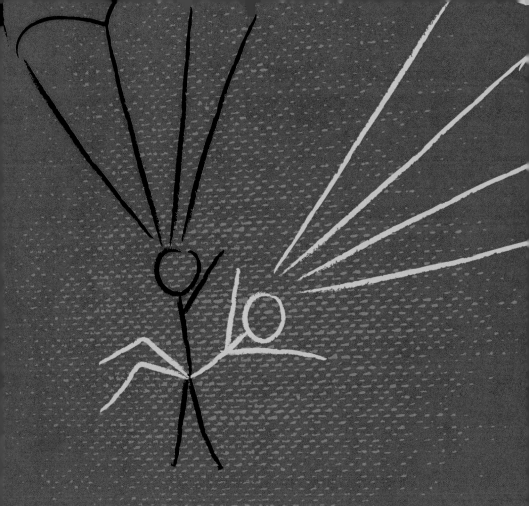

GET READY FOR A HARD LANDING
(wink wink)

36 | **Mile High Club**

37   **Riding Bareback**

Tight spin and a perfect landing

38 An Olympic '10'

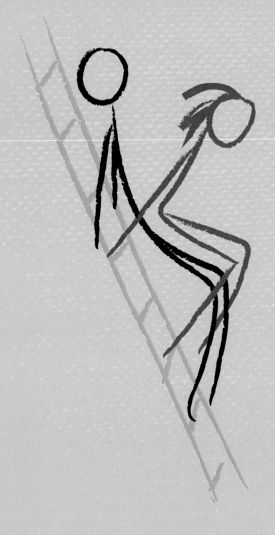

39 Snakes and Ladders

Very familiar
with beavers

40   The Canadian

41 Oval Office

Feels good on so many levels
(Especially on floors 6 and 9)

42 **The Shaft**

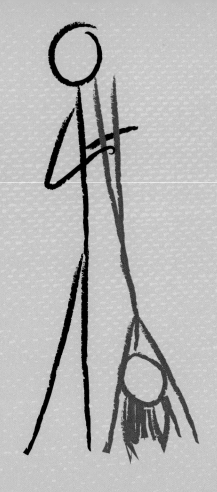

Stands tall and erect

43 **Eiffel Tower**

BEWARE OF:
- sand
- crabs
- a salty surprise

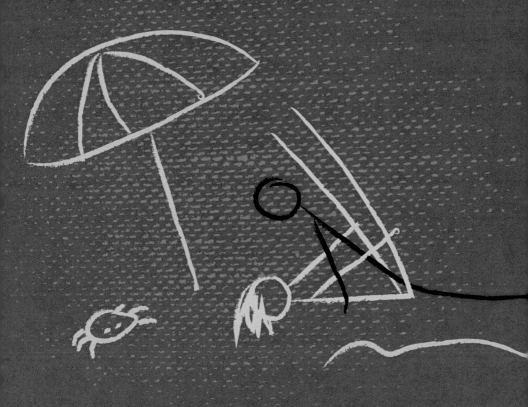

44 The Clam Digger

BONER OF STEEL

45 The Hero

Made in the USA
Middletown, DE
08 September 2023